Europe

by Mike Graf

Consultant:
Catherine H. Helgeland
Professor of Geography
University of Wisconsin–Manitowoc
Manitowoc, Wisconsin

Bridgestone Books
an imprint of Capstone Press
Mankato, Minnesota

Bridgestone Books are published by Capstone Press
151 Good Counsel Drive, P.O. Box 669, Mankato, Minnesota 56002
http://www.capstone-press.com

Library of Congress Cataloging-in-Publication Data
Graf, Mike.
    Europe/by Mike Graf.
    p. cm.—(Continents)
    Summary: A very brief introduction to the geography, various regions, natural
resources, people, and wildlife of Europe.
    Includes bibliographical references and index.
    ISBN 0-7368-1418-3 (hardcover)
    1. Europe—Juvenile literature. [1. Europe] I. Title. II. Continents (Mankato, Minn.)
D900 .G7 2003
914–dc21   2002000208

Editorial Credits

Erika Mikkelson, editor; Karen Risch, product planning editor, Linda Clavel, designer and
    illustrator; Image Select International, photo researchers

Photo Credits

Art Directors and TRIP/H. Rogers, 11; T. Bognar, 13; P. Mercea, 15
Bruce Chashin/Index Stock Imagery/PictureQuest, 19
CORBIS/Macduff Everton, 17; Tim Thompson, 20; Chris Rainier, 22 (fjord); Morton Beebe, 22
    (Checkpoint Charlie)
Digital Stock, 22 (Stonehenge)
Digital Wisdom/Mountain High, cover
Martin Ruegner/Pictor International, Ltd./PictureQuest, 21

1 2 3 4 5 6 07 06 05 04 03 02

Table of Contents

Fast Facts about Europe

Population: About 699 million

Number of countries: 43

Largest cities: Moscow, Russia; London, United Kingdom; Paris, France

Highest point: Mount Elbrus, 18,510 feet (5,642 meters) high

Lowest point: surface of the Caspian Sea, 92 feet (28 meters) below sea level

Longest river: Volga River, 2,293 miles (3,689 kilometers)

Countries in Europe

1. Iceland	23. Austria
2. Ireland	24. Hungary
3. United Kingdom	25. Slovenia
4. Netherlands	26. Croatia
5. Belgium	27. Bosnia and Herzegovina
6. Luxembourg	
7. France	28. Yugoslavia
8. Portugal	29. Macedonia
9. Spain	30. Albania
10. Andorra	31. Greece
11. Monaco	32. Bulgaria
12. Switzerland	33. Romania
13. Denmark	34. Moldova
14. Germany	35. Ukraine
15. Liechtenstein	36. Russia
16. Italy	37. Belarus
17. San Marino	38. Lithuania
18. Vatican City	39. Latvia
19. Malta	40. Estonia
20. Poland	41. Finland
21. Czech Republic	42. Sweden
22. Slovakia	43. Norway

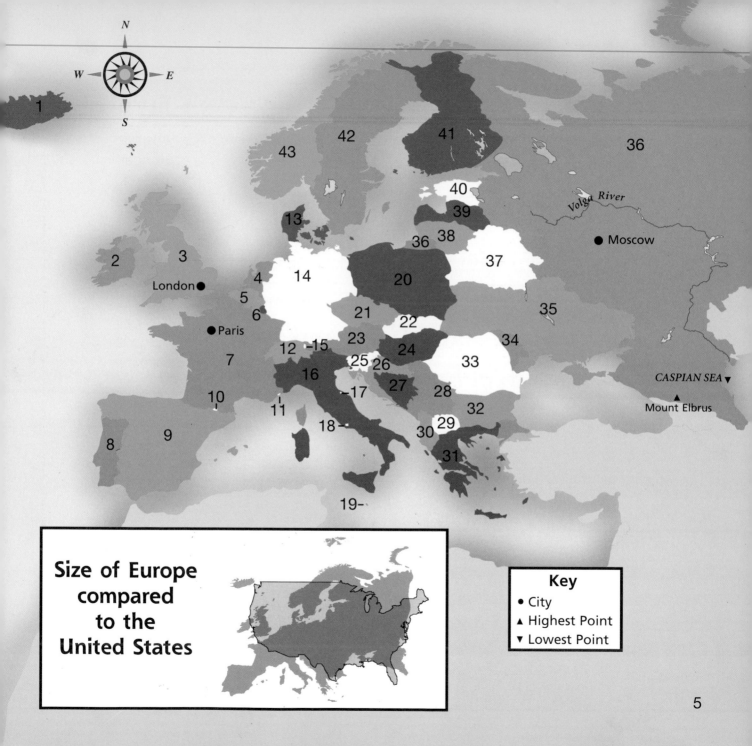

N

W   E

S

1

2   3

43

42

36

41

Volga River

40

39

13

36   38

● Moscow

37

London ●

4

14

20

35

5

21

33

22

6

London ●

Paris ●

12 —15

23

24

34

7

25

26

● Moscow

33

CASPIAN SEA ▼

16

—17

27

28

32

Mount Elbrus ▲

10

11

18 —

30   29

8

9

31

19 —

**Size of Europe
compared
to the
United States**

Key

● City
▲ Highest Point
▼ Lowest Point

5

Europe

Europe is the sixth largest continent. The Atlantic Ocean is west of Europe. Asia lies to the east. The Mediterranean Sea and Africa are south of Europe. The Arctic Ocean is north of Europe.

ARCTIC OCEAN

ATLANTIC OCEAN

MEDITERRANEAN SEA

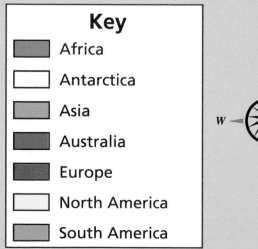

Key

Africa

Antarctica

Asia

Australia

Europe

North America

South America

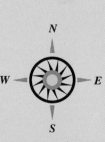

N

W   E

S

Europe's Land

Europe has many mountain ranges. The Alps spread across several European countries. The Carpathian Mountains are in eastern Europe. The Pyrenees Mountains are in southern Europe. They separate France from Spain.

range
a chain or large group of mountains

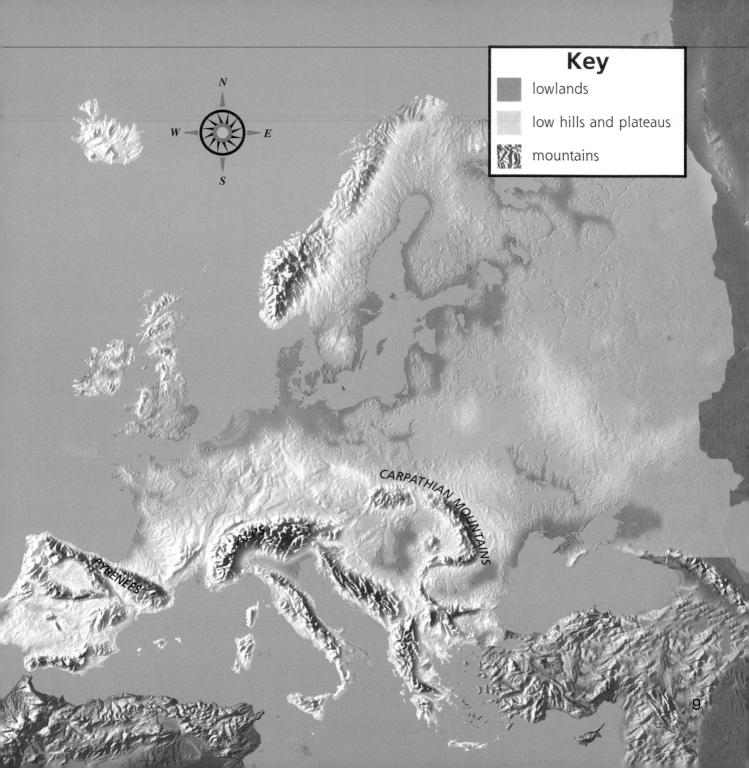

Key
- lowlands
- low hills and plateaus
- mountains

CARPATHIAN MOUNTAINS

ALPS

PYRENEES

9

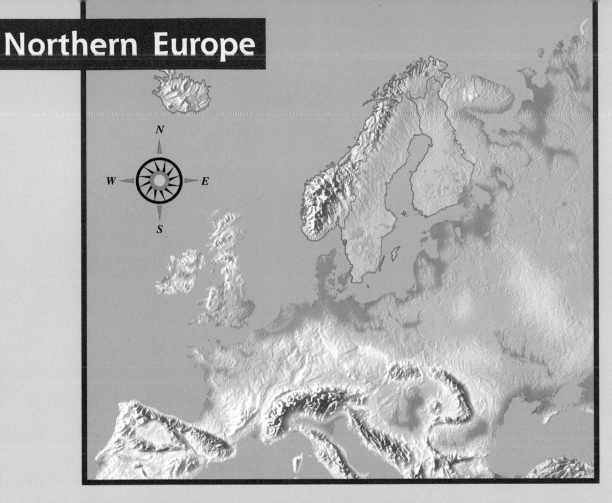

The climate is cold in far northern Europe.
In winter, the sun shines for only a few hours
each day. In summer, the sun never sets.

climate

the usual weather in a place

glacier in Iceland

Many people catch fish off northern Europe's coasts. Iceland is an island in northern Europe. It has both volcanoes and large glaciers.

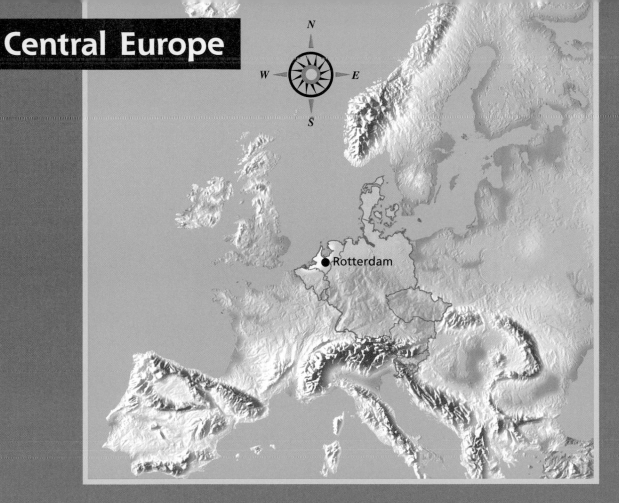

Germany and the Netherlands are countries in central Europe. Germany is one of Europe's most important makers of cars.

Rotterdam, Netherlands

Rotterdam, Netherlands, is a port city on the Rhine River in central Europe. The port ships more cargo than any other port in the world.

port
a place where ships can load and unload goods

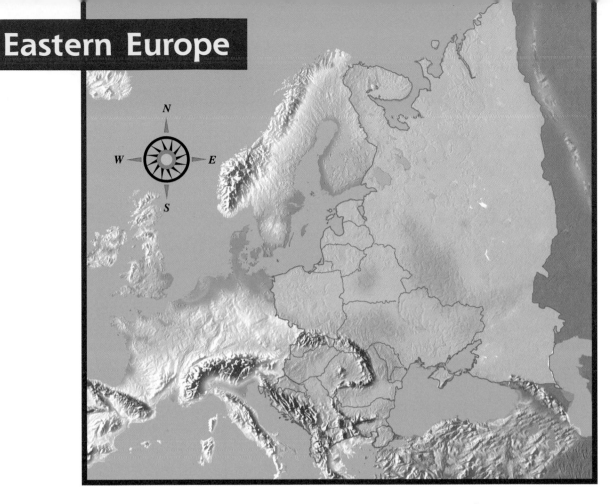

Eastern Europe has many natural resources. People in Poland and Ukraine make steel from the coal and iron ore found there.

Some people in eastern Europe farm without machines. Farmers instead use horses and oxen.

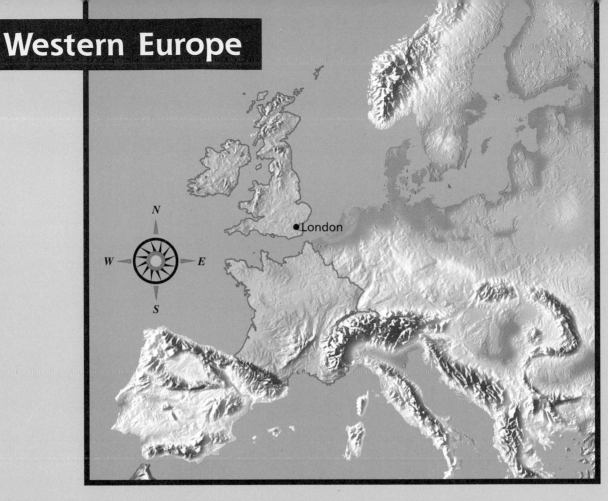

London

France, Switzerland, and the United Kingdom are in western Europe. Vineyards grow in France and Switzerland. People make wine from grapes grown in vineyards.

London,
England

London, England, is the largest city in the United Kingdom. About 7 million people live there.

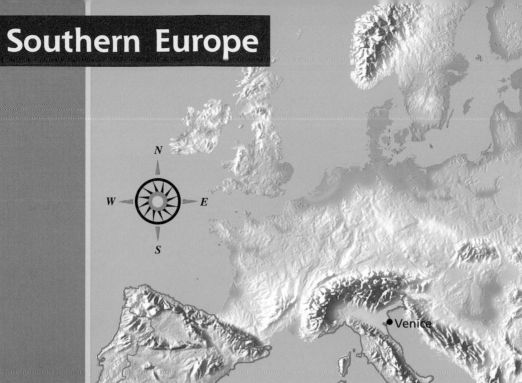

Italy, Greece, and Spain are countries in southern Europe. Many tourists travel to these countries. They enjoy the warm climate there.

London,
England

London, England, is the largest city in the
United Kingdom. About 7 million people
live there.

Venice

Italy, Greece, and Spain are countries in southern Europe. Many tourists travel to these countries. They enjoy the warm climate there.

Venice, Italy

Venice, Italy, is built on islands in a lagoon.
People travel through the city in boats
called gondolas.

lagoon

a shallow pool of seawater
separated from the sea by a
narrow strip of land

19

Europe's forests, mountains, and waters are home to many animals. Swans and ducks nest near lakes and ponds.

Bears, wolves, and foxes make their homes in forests. Falcons and eagles nest high in the mountains.

Reading Maps: Europe's Sights to See

1. Stonehenge is a stone formation in the United Kingdom. Ancient people placed these huge stones there about 4,000 years ago. If you were to travel west from Stonehenge, which ocean would you reach? Use the map on page 7 to answer this question.

2. Many fjords are found in northern Europe. A fjord is a long, narrow inlet of water between high cliffs. Norway has many fjords along its coast. In which direction would you travel to reach Spain from Norway? Use the map on page 5 to answer this question.

3. The Berlin Wall was built in 1961. It separated East and West Berlin, Germany. East Germany and West Germany became one country in 1990. Checkpoint Charlie is a museum located where the wall once stood. In which direction would you travel from Berlin, Germany, to reach the Alps? Use the maps on pages 5 and 9 to answer this question.

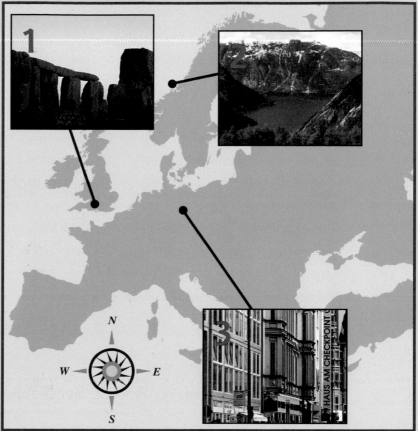

Words to Know

ancient (AYN-shunt)—from a time long ago
cargo (KAR-goh)—the goods carried by a ship, truck, or aircraft
fjord (FYORD)—a long, narrow bay of ocean between high cliffs
glacier (GLAY-shur)—a huge mass of slowly moving ice
gondola (GON-duh-luh)—a light boat with high, pointed ends used to move through the water
vineyard (VIN-yurd)—an area of land where grapes are grown
volcano (vol-KAY-noh)—a mountain with vents; a vent is a passage that goes deep into the Earth; melted rock, ash, and gases erupt through the vents.

Read More

Foster, Leila Merrell. *Europe.* Continents. Chicago: Heinemann, 2001.
Fowler, Allan. *Europe.* Rookie Read-About Geography. New York: Children's Press, 2001.
Petersen, David. *Europe.* A True Book. New York: Children's Press, 1998.

Internet Sites

CIA Kids Page—Geography
http://www.cia.gov/cia/ciakids/geography
Geo World—World Geography and Climates
http://www.kbears.com/siteonesilent/geographiebon.html
NationalGeographic.com—MapMachine
http://plasma.nationalgeographic.com/mapmachine/
   facts_fs.html

Index